Sifting Through The Sand

ANELA LANI

Foreword by Victor Alumbaugh

Copyright © 2017 Anela Lani

All rights reserved.

ISBN: 0692965882
ISBN-13: 978-0-692-96588-7

Edited by Daniel B. Martin
Front & back cover photos by Vanessa Lilly

DEDICATION

Dedicated to my flightless bird.

Anela Lani

PARTS

Foreword	i
Acknowledgments	iv
1 Shifting Sands	Pg. 1
2 Salt & Light	Pg. 70

FOREWORD

"The yearning to know what cannot be known, to comprehend the incomprehensible, to touch and taste the unapproachable, arises from the image of God in the nature of man. Deep calleth unto deep, and though polluted and landlocked by the mighty disaster theologians call the Fall, the soul senses its origin and longs to return to its source."

-A.W. Tozer

I am in constant awe at the transformation of a soul returning to its source. On more than one occasion I've encountered, the same as most of you, a soul longing for its purpose. Maybe your coworker, maybe your boss, maybe your closest friend, maybe the person sitting next to you at a bar or in a pew, it makes no difference. I've noticed a certain longing in a man's being that aches for meaning. A soul that cries out in deafening silence; stubborn refusal to believe that mankind are merely creatures of accident or coincidence. The more open minded of us have come to accept a belief of a supernatural force or forces at work in our day to day lives. We've had occurrences that make no sense logically but something inside of us cries out in agreement: "Truth!" We can try to rationalize it, but we can't seem to fit it in any of the boxes we've made, we can try to ignore it but we can't ignore the peace we felt when it came. If you're like myself, you can try to ponder it to some level of belief that makes "normal" people slowly back away from you, but the reality is this: something shifted, reality as we knew it was turned on its head and the impossible, improbable, & irrational suddenly forced its way into our world and refused to rest in any of our "boxes."

A majority of the world today believe in God, gods, or the concept of God, for the very reason that they refuse to consider themselves "all-knowing" & for the fact that they know they've had an encounter that they just couldn't wrap their brain around. In humility, they stopped trying to, and in this same humility they opened themselves up to a new dimension of reality that was beyond logical.

I've watched Anela go through the phases described and search through spiritual book after spiritual book for something that could satisfy the longing in her soul. I believe every human will at some point in their life develop this same "hunger" and choose to suppress or pursue it, some to satisfaction, & others to endless searching. I've met people who've traveled to the corners of the world to "find themselves", trying different techniques to achieve that inner peace that seems to be so fleeting. I personally believe, that if there was a God and there was indeed a rest for our longing souls, a place where our hearts could nest in peace eternally, a place where we could call 'home' regardless of where we might be geographically, this God or gods or forces or whatever you want to call it wouldn't be so cruel as to make this "haven", this "sanctuary" so close yet so out of reach that one must wander years upon years in pursuit of this place only to find that it is ever fleeting.

My belief is if there was such a place, and if we agree that all eventually have this inward longing for said place, then this place mustn't be so "out of our reach" as we think. I believe it's closer than we know.

Anela paints a beautiful picture of a heart longing for meaning, of a soul searching for its source through effort and striving only to discover the home she left as a child was the same home she spent years searching out. I am overwhelmed at the transformation that Anela went through in her "search". There is a noticeably stirring anointing upon the second half of this book. A shift in voice and heart. There is a hope that has come alive on the pages. I realized I was no longer reading the words of another human being. There was an inspired overlapping that I couldn't shake: This was a new creation!

I hope this book will put your doubts at rest, silence those accusing thoughts of insanity (you're not crazy), put a stop to the endless search, and lead you home.

- Victor Alumbaugh

ACKNOWLEDGMENTS

I would like to thank every person that has been a part of my life, for no matter how short a time or to what extent. Each interaction was and still is an ingredient in all of my writing. Most importantly, I give thanks to God, my mother who is my rock, my father who always believed we can do anything, my brother, Victor, who guides me through this beautiful spiritual journey, my sister, Ana, whose grace and strength has made my trust deeper, my sister, Pele, whose wisdom and lightheartedness has brightened my days, and my youngest brother Koa, whose intelligence and passion for life has assured me that there is so much hope for the future.

SHIFTING SANDS

Poetry & Testimony

In the heat of early morning
With the sunrise facing us,
The sand glittered,
Calling to my eyes.

I stopped to give it my attention
And it was then I knew,
He was going to teach me a lesson
From which I grew and grew.

In Light

The sun cannot ask for forgiveness
From those whom he burns.
He is there without will
And he shines his brightest,
Facing one direction.

The sun cannot ask for forgiveness
From those who see darkness.
He cannot reach all ends of the earth
And he shines his brightest,
Facing one direction.

You have to understand,
He doesn't know why.

Tips For Kindness

Don't ever question *style*.
Don't ever question anything
That gives meaning to a smile.

Think, Act

A lovely personification of an object surreal,
Does not compare to what humans feel.

In spite of the pain and anguish at times,
A lovely mimic is an unpleasant mime.

Between the hardships and easy ships galore,
Exists a state of ecstasy you cannot ignore.

A lovely idea intrudes the mind,
Until human reaction begins to unwind.

Duel Of Courage

I'm an ocean of emotion,
But a river flows in me.

> I have all the power in my self,
> To be who I aim to be…
> But you keep bringing me down,
> Pulling my thoughts from out of the clouds.
>
> Can't you see?

I'm an ocean of emotion,
But a river flows in me.

Little Me

i never seem to be satisfied with where i am

because I've got Big Dreams and even Bigger Plans
because I've got Aspirations and Other Worldly Ideas

but i've got limitations and limiting fears.
in a messy mind stands blockades of dust,
made of confused faces and misplaced lusts.

i never seem to be satisfied with where i am

because I've got Big Dreams and even Bigger Plans

Now, Here & The Little Worlds

There are times when I sit
And stall at my rest stop.
Out of the car,
I am focused on what I am doing
And what is surrounding me.

I become captivated in this Little World.
So much so, that I forget it is just a world in a
Cluster of many worlds.

So I gather my value-ables,
Throw away the trash I don't need,
And get back on the road.

While driving, I find peace.

I remember, while gazing off
Into the blur of a distance,

That the journey is always the best part.

Rainbow

There goes my heart,
Bold as love.
So below, as above!
High with the tides
And down with the sea.
Into the blue,
Then green with envy.

Violet spectrum
Of awareness, I try.
I climb ladders
Of colors, as my
Red makes me cry.
Enemies close,
Like white is to black.
Help me, rainbow,
Paint the picture I lack.

It Is

I feel an odd dislike for "it may."
It's unknowing and befuddling,
Such a bold thing to say.

> I feel a close relation with how you say "it may."
> It's a statement with a shadow.
> A fact, to my dismay.

I feel like when I hear "it may"
It rather shouldn't be.

> But rather be "it is,
> Of course!
> Of my most certainty!"

Excusé Moi

If I'm going to be misunderstood for most of my life,
Let it be at my will.

If I'm going to be wronged more than I'm right,
Let me pay the bill.

If I'm going to run into walls,
While chasing after my dreams,

Let me take on the sorrow and shame,
For nothing's ever as it seems.

Amoré

There's a tune that will never fade for as long as I shall live.
Should amnesia find me with old age,
The moon will always
Bring
Me
Back.

You mustn't think too hard on why things in life
Are as they are,
For you'll almost
Always
Go
Mad.

Storm

It was only through hurt
That my soul began to see,
The dissonance and fallacies
In my reality.

And only through pain
Was I blessed to heal,
Opening my consciousness
To the rarity of real.

Trust Me

Trust me this means something!
I swear it does!
It isn't just a poem or words that almost rhyme.
At the same time,
Maybe it is.

The fact that words traveled from her mind to yours,
Is the ultimate evidence of the ultimate tour.
Trust me this means something!
I don't just like to repeat…

But there's something so beautiful about a circular feat.

Ms. Lonely

Learn how to make yourself laugh.
That way if you ever end up alone,
At least you'll be happy.

Dark

If you ever catch me staring for a second too long or
Not smiling because I think too much…
I'm taking in all of the moment,
Breathing in reality with my special touch.

What I can hear from every person
And what I hear as I walk by,
It's the pull that moves me along,
Movement in the corner of my eye.

The moment is a memory, but why this moment?

Sometimes life surprises you with a certain simplicity
You can't help but hold.

No reason, no motive,
Replayed when you're old.

Planted

How wondrous it must be,
To be a plant rooted in the ground.
To be an observer of the chaos,
Watching without a sound.

To be awakened by the sun,
And fed by the rain.
To feel one's growth
As the world grows the same.

How wondrous it must be,
To be a flower in the soil,
Free from humanly drama, heartbreak,
Disappointment and turmoil.

Hold Me

Heaven just might be,
Being comfortable,
Without inhibition,
In one moment,
For a very long time.

Hard Season

My soul aches for you
And the pain you suffer through.
This battle is for life,
And it's been a rough start,
Between your conflicting actions
And the good in your heart.

You have made us stronger.
You've helped us to see,
How much we need each other
More than in daunting disparity.

Our love continues to grow,
But warp and mold and change.
Still, it's love everlasting,
Heightened by something so deranged.

There are many questions
That leave us hanging here.
It's hard to keep your head straight
When you're accustomed to fear.

I thought I saw you die once
And the moment was surreal.
My whole world collapsed,
I did not know what to feel.

Sifting Through The Sand

But in that same moment,
I realized this is how it's going to be,
Always on our toes,
Walking through life carefully.

I can't imagine the horror
That goes on in those little heads,
I can only hope to save them
From the trauma and the dread.

I can only wish to help heal them,
Be there when they need.
I can only hope they'll be okay
Growing with this poison seed.

This delusion does something to the mind,
Which is difficult to understand.
We love you, need you, pray for you,
But we're sinking in quicksand.

We're all a little broken,
While we glue each other whole.
Every event is a new misery
Only in God, can we console.

Perspectiva

When
Things
Are
Bad
Remember,

They could be
Much worse.

The Sometimes Switch

Sometimes I switch perspectives,
To entertain my mind.
Like seeing with no audio
Or listening while blind.
Sometimes I switch perspectives,
To enliven reality.
What if we're experiments
A holy scientist oversees?
Sometimes I switch perspectives,
To even out the game
If I was an ant…
Would I,
Or my mother have a name?
Sometimes I switch perspectives,
Because in life,
I think I'd like to know
All the different ways, in which,
The unpaved paths may go.

Quiet

There's a young man in the middle of a crowded room
Who plays out different scenes in his head.
How can he start a conversation?
    With his neighbor,
        His old friend,
           With anybody,
              Anywhere,
                  Willing to listen?

We are all connected,
Not by our inability to connect
But by our desire to.

Discussion

He asked her,
        "Can I bounce some ideas off you?"
She replied
        "Sure, got a ball?"
I laughed in quiet
At the boy with the shoe,
Who couldn't seem to tie it.
The lace was clean,
But the sole was worn.
He said,
        "These ideas are where greatness is born!"
So he bounced back home,
Around the corner,
And down the street.
While the girl stood there smiling,
With no shoes on her feet.

Sometimes he who is found,
Had no idea he was missing.

Whatever You Do…

Whatever you do,
Don't stop learning!

Don't stop reading and finding new books,
Sit outside on the grass and get hooked!

Don't stop looking up the facts you want to know,
Sit outside on a bench and watch the day go!

Don't stop searching for the clues you think exist,
Sit outside and look at all the things you've missed!

Don't stop asking and never fear to ask again,
Evil are those who want curiosity to end!

But, You Can.

Life is a waking dream
And you are so small,
So do the impossible
And live big and tall.

Life is a lucid dream
And you certainly can't fly,
So do the unthinkable
And kiss the sky.

Life is a globe in space
And you are a cloud of dust,
So do the unpredictable and

Keep
Dreaming,
You
Must!

If I Left Tomorrow

I won't regret not seeing Paris
& all the places I could have flown.
It won't kill me that I didn't go to Fiji,
Africa or Rome.

What will hang heavy on my heart,
& echo in my soul?

The words left unsaid,
& the love left untold.

Traveler

Sometimes you just want to drop everything
And run.
Say fuck it and fly away.
But you have to be patient,
You have to plan it out.
So in your patience,
You grasp onto anything
That reminds you that you are alive.
And you make decisions
That you think you can get away with,
Because the impatience starts to eat at your soul.
And you can't even sit in your skin.
And you can't be alone with your thoughts.
Numbing.
Dumbing.
Can't wait to start running.

I'm going to get pounded into the ground,
A little while longer,
Then,
I run.

Questions

I've heard stories of the after life,
The beauty in one's death,
The journey to eternity,
The imagery in your head.

Does heaven exist in our mind?
As when we close our eyes that one last time,
Do we enter the final dream we have been anticipating?

Is heaven but a dimension created in your thoughts,
Formulated by your life,
An experience of all your positivity?
Does our afterlife reside in the subconscious we "cannot"
Fully grab a hold of while awake?

And hell, if heaven is such,
Would be the negativity we fail to escape.
Our perception of what is evil,
Doesn't that conjure up this fear?
If hell is the worst place to be, what elements of your
World are the worst to you?
Do we overcome this potential underworld
By rising above our fears?

I'm hoping my heart stops beating only
When my mind is at peace.
But why must death concern me,
As long as I'm alive?

Warning

You already know what you should do.
Just keep praying for the courage to do it.

18 Years Old

I need to stop caring about what people think.
I think pretty soon I'm going to call up that shrink.
Should I write a book about poems and such?
Shel Silverstein inspired, with a teenager's touch?
I don't know if that'd sell and I don't know if I'd have
Big enough balls to put my words out for laughs…
Maybe I should get started, maybe this is it…
It does seem smart, now that I think about it.

So here I go, maybe this is the first page.
A book about: How I Can't Get Past This Stage,
Of not knowing what to do
And which way to turn.
I'm ready to grow up
And I'm ready to learn.
But I need some guidance,
And definitely some help!
This is the most confused,
I've ever
Felt.

Dedication Kit

Do you know what,
I've been thinking?
Because when I do, I start sinking.
I feel it spread through my soul
And I know, I'm close to losing control.

But if you saw me really,
I may be acting silly,
Cuz I'm lost, friend,
But you found me.
Then you held my breath
And drowned me.
Underwater,
So deep.
Your memory's all I keep.
So I sing these songs to breathe
I'll paint you on my sleeve.

Do you know what,
I've been thinking?
'Cuz when I do, I start drinking.
Now, I feel it spread through my soul.
Yeah, I know…
I'm out of control.

Regret

It should never be about money.

It should be about doing all the things
You've fantasized.
So when that day comes,
& you're laying on your deathbed,
You don't whisper to yourself,

"I should've."

It's Simple Pt. 1

To be happy: be grateful,
For what you have & have not.

Remember what becomes of you
Is all an afterthought.

Surprise

don't be surprised when I create things
that you did not know to exist,
because a lot of me hides in my mind's corner
I call the abyss.

a box of trinkets I buried when I was ten,
a poem I wrote in love,
a book I read that showed me
how my life is far from tough,
a stuffed animal shaped like a sheep,
and a picture of my first kiss,

a lot of me hides in my mind's corner
I call the abyss.

Intellectuals

Listen when they speak.
Does it sound like an echo?
Ideology mixologists!
You've just got to let go.

Ask me why,
And I'll tell you this:
Everyone's a genius
When ignorance is bliss.

Fuel the fire,
Just to put it out.
All of these general ideas,
Until you grasp *what it's about*.

But will you ever get it?
And do they really know?
Illusionary visionaries,
Always putting on a show.

Writers

If I could,
I would,
Feel the thoughts
That spin through your head,
Leading you to
The sheets on my bed.

Then caress the words,
You compose out of wreck,
Breathing you in
With each taste of your neck.

Textual

Blinking cursor haunting.
Why are you the same speed as my heart?
A mirror pulse of my indecisiveness,
A drum roll for my mistakes.

Blinking cursor haunting.
Taunting and ridicule from an object?
I won't allow it.
Dating really sucks.

Reveal myself to me,
Blinking cursor ghost.
Making me feel like I caught feelings,
Starting a war with your own host.

Blinking cursor haunting,
Of the things I could have said.
You make me think,
Chivalry cloned itself in AI and pronounced itself dead.

Puppy Love

If you know this love,
You know that nothing can compare.
Lust, the rush of mysterious attractions,
And blinded interactions,
Can't live up to the feeling you get
When you know it's real.
You don't have to question
How the other feels.

It's the difference between letting it breath,
And trying to figure out
If you like what you see.

You know how it feels to need
Nothing but one person,
That you can talk to
And know for certain,
They'll always be there.
Despite the pain,
You know they care.

If you know this love,
You know it's innocent,
Beautiful,
And hard to find.
Even when you're not searching,
She's on your mind.

4:30 a.m.

When in a daze,
I don't watch the days last.
What I did yesterday is now in the past.
The past in my trash, about to get emptied.
I don't think of those times,
But time,
I've got plenty.

The moments that occur and the words that connect,
Don't give myself a chance to reflect.
Still in a daze, at a slowed pace,
Keeping me here, I can't leave this place.
I've gone too far to think about that,
Left too much, to want you back.
What was right to me, is out the door,
I dropped those promises on the floor.

Frankly, it won't be the same.
I put my thoughts in a haze.
I did not watch or start to stop,
Our chapter as it set ablaze.

Not a breath to relax.
No savior to call.
Choices revealed, destroying it all.
Still in a daze, I am not me.
Or who you figured,
I used to be.

Cycle

She was lost in a world full of choices.
Carried herself with a head full of voices.
She strayed,
Far from the norm.
Walked nowhere,
Without pausing to mourn.

Catapult

This is how love sometimes works:

Like a catapult,
You're pulled further and further back,
      Into the deepest,
      Least ventured,
      Parts of yourself.
      And reality closes in on you,
Becoming a shrinking perspective
The farther back you're pulled.

      Then, there's an instant.

You stop to find your world strained.
You rest calmly in the hands of another,
With no control
Of what happens

      When they let go.

Seconds I can't Unsee

When my father told me
I was only three.
I bled, we fled
Part of me grew up,
Part of me dead.

And after my first "real" time,
An imagined love story,
Turned nightmare
When he called it statutory.

There was the school trip,
And the boy I didn't like
Who knocked, tricked, entered
And made me put up a fight.

The last time, though,
I was in love,
So I was blind to understand,
No means No
Not, if you try hard enough, you can.

Seconds I can't unsee,
Faces I won't forget.
Animal eyes in humans,
Possessed,
While evil seeped through sweat.

Window Pain

Have you ever watched raindrops run down a window?
One drop at the top begins to slowly drip down,
Absorbing the other raindrops in it's path,
Making itself a bigger drop.
And the more drops it encounters,
The heavier this drop becomes.
Thus, the faster it falls.
Sometimes, I am like this drop,
Taking on more than I can carry.
And sometimes, I bring on more than I can hold onto
With the center of my gravity.

Like that heavy drop,
I fall pretty fast,
When my burden
Outweighs my capabilities.

Future

As I grow older, I wonder where I'll be.
I ask myself, what will I be doing?
And who will I marry?
Hours pass me by,
And they soon become days,
But I still wonder where my future lays.
I carry on the week, as I do what I please,
Most of what I need,
Unwritten memories tease.

I look forward to the present and the morning after next,
And think really hard as I type this text…
Where will I be five years from now?
What will be my point of view?
Will I still believe the old?
Or something totally new?
Everyone I meet,
Will effect my train of thought.
The words they spill into my ears,
Will leave me sort of caught.
Thinking what's the better way,
The way I think or them?
As I listen closely, I decide my future on a whim.
I guess I'm living proof of history,
And the days about to come.
Who else will write my extraordinary story
Of who I am and where I'm from?

Anela Lani

Heads Up

Being a young adult,
You start questioning everything,
And contradicting yourself constantly.

Insta Fame

Who are you when no one's looking?
And when you've got no one to see?
Who is it that you talk to,
When you're not being
Who you're trying to be?

To get lost in an image
Of a life that's not your own,
Is an absolute tragedy,
You have given up your throne.

Friday Night Fairy Tales

On the off chance that someone may be interested in you,
Because of those eyes,
Or because of those lips…
How about we make it easier?
Show them a piercing,
Or a flash of your hips,
Or a tattoo that tells,
Or one that needs answers.
Out and about,
Where we're all just dancers.

On the off chance that it might be your smile,
What makes you wonder, what makes him worth while?

It must be my body,
My skin, and my hair,
The dress I have on, that shows my despair.
No.

I know for sure, it was my smile,
That got them started,
That brought them this mile.
That gave them the bravery,
To walk up to me
And courageously ask,
If I'd willing to be…
No.

Sifting Through The Sand

On the off chance that it was my words,
And he hung onto every
Enchanting
Syllable he heard…
No.

I'll just walk away and guess that it wasn't,
Because a fairy tale on a Friday night?
It just doesn't.

W.W.

Wednesday wisdom,
Some midweek motivation.
The middle of the week,
When you're feeling low on inspiration.
When Monday and Tuesday have gone,
But the week still has some time.
Hump day happiness
Is not a crime.

There is never growth in comfort,
And never comfort in growth,
But there is a still beauty
That exists in both.

Middle of the week blues,
Joyful hope combatting sadness.
Revel in the future
And sulk in the gladness.

Lift your glasses,
Toast to friends and drinking wine.
Live in the moment you were placed in
And know that you will be just fine.

I think therefore I drink

There's an awkward euphoria I have
The morning after.
It's full of nonsense
And nonstop laughter.
I love it and hate it,
In the same breadth of time.
But I ponder so hard,
It blows my mind…

Today,
I realized
Why I drink.
It's simply because,

I over think.

Well Within

I brought a bucket to the well of wisdom & behold,
I fell in…

Finding myself trapped in a conundrum of
Learning from within.

Escape

I don't want to be a distraction.
Just call me your escape.
And if you need a partner,
I'm down to be your date.
And if you'd like a kiss,
I can give you that too.
I don't have to be in love,
To have fun with you.

When we're long distance,
I won't call in vain.
Cell phones were invented
To drive lovers insane.

Tick Tock Candy Shop

A playback forgotten,
Stuck in a rewind.
With eyes closed soft
And a touch of divine.
If this loops once more,
I don't think I can stand it.
Love, loss, repeat,
Apologetic relationship bandit.

There's not enough time.
Caught in a clock.
There's never enough open hours
In the candy shop.
If only seconds could stop!
At my command.
And two bodies working as one,
Could make time stand.

Mesmerized by the illusion of time.
What measures this place?
Your mind or mine?

Cookie Jar

Guilty pleasures,
Like cookies in a jar.
Looks like bliss
But won't get you far.
Feels pretty good,
When you finally get a taste.
Then worthless
And gone,
Quickly to waste.
Guilty pleasures,
Entice you with temptation.
Only for a moment,
To feed that fixation,
And when you're satisfied,

It's done.

You can lay yourself to sleep,
And think about that cookie,
You didn't have to eat.

We're all selfish creatures
On the hunt for happiness.

Sick

Lovesick, sick of lust.
Caring for you,
Way too much.
What's the easiest way to tell you
That this heart has cut strings?
Like a free vein,
I detached from those things.

Theres no easy way to let this be.
I want you to be happy,
Without me.
I'll listen to the song you sent
One hundred times.
Though the lyrics hit hard and shut my mouth
In reality, I know, we only head south.
I'm not willing to connect,
And not willing to call.
I miss you sometimes
But not us at all.

Dive

I met him on a misty morning,
Wet picnic table.
Hands held his face,
So unstable.
He led me to the edge
And pointed to blue.
All I could wonder was
Who did this to you?

Where is your love?
Where is your old soul?
He had it all and I watched him let it go.

He said,
"There down deep,
At the bottom of the sea,
But you're the only one
Who would dive for me."

"Dating"

I'm convinced our hearts are fragile,
So I'll treat them as such.

Let's stay at a safe distance,
While we dream of the touch.

Altered Atmosphere

Cornered in a room,
I'm surrounded by peers.
Familiar faces, I've known,
For so many years.

A presence appears and it
Rests on my back.
One that I've missed
And recognize like a fact.

The warmth wraps my body,
From my feet to my face.
When it enters my mind
I remember a place…
Where love once existed
And all my worries relaxed.
Your company alone,
Seems to take me back.

Insomniac

I'd be up for hours
Thinking about this night.
Writing down my thoughts,
Weighing wrong from right.

I'd be up for days on end,
Eating little of real food.
Emotions are enough,
To feed this frenzy named my mood.

I'd be up for hours,
Because minutes fly by like air.
On these nights,
I will show myself,
How to live with you not there.

Foreseer

I used to miss your company
And the comfort that came,
With the wide smiles
And the jokes that were lame.
I loved your energy
When you were at your best,
But I didn't appreciate you enough,
To love you during the rest.

I believed that one day, you'd meet a girl
That loves you for you,
That you could give all
Of your care and trust to.

I'm sorry I played
All those childish games,
And I'm sorry for the things
I didn't mean to say.
I miss the talks
And knowing we could relate.
But feelings ventured
Through love, then hate.
I recall being unstable
And wrecking my brain
And keeping it real
While being insane.

Super Nova

When we came together,
My old star met yours.
In the sky we touched,
Like it happened once before.

A cataclysmic crash,
Two supernovas became one.
Then God gave us life lessons,
After we had our fun.

And like the dying stars we are,
We began to burn out, as they do.
Bright and fast, then dim and dull
When intentions were untrue.

The Break Down

Relations
With another being
Two minds collide
Four eyes, no seeing.

Emotions
Choking the atmosphere
Apparent to a couple
Two waves of fear.

Words
Exchanged without thought
Reassembled from sense
Used while they fought.

Pain
No longer around
Dug deep into scars
Not wanting to be found.

Ends
Where they both met
Two years in an instance
Too real to forget.

Discovery

The better I get to know myself,
The deeper I dive.
& The deeper I go,
The scarier it gets.
Like the ocean,
At it's depths,
It gets colder
& darker.
But at the bottom,
A strange peace awaits you.

Youngin'

The future is beautiful because I pave my own path.
I dream of solutions and carefully do the math.
The human mind is power and without it,
We would dissolve.
All of the problems which arise in the world,
A tiny brain can solve.

What I want is happiness,
I believe that so do all.
I wish I could gather some
& pass it out as smiles fall.

If the world were ending soon
And I had some time to spare,
I'd spend it with the people of whom I really care.
I'd gather everyone and tell them how I feel.
I'd tear down my wall of secrets and finally be real.
I'd cry for the whole time and spill out tears of joy.
I'd look truth in the eye and not tell a single lie.

Tomorrow could be the last,
And all that we know may be gone,
But I want to leave it right,
Even though I've lived some wrong.

Sand Slipped

I felt electric in my bones,
Energy in my skin.
It was a power greater than me
That made me take you in.
It was a rush of something else,
Not many get to see.
It was a surge of gravity,
The core right under me.

I felt full surrender.
Total engraved body shock.
I recorded every moment,
Every time I heard you talk.
I recall so clearly,
Yet it's still a mystery.

How could I let it be?
It was a surge of gravity,
The core right under me.

Reaching

God.
I carry on my shoulders
About three thousand pounds,
Of emptiness and sadness
That I wish I hadn't found.

Sometimes I feel your hand,
Pressing on my chest,
As to knock me down,
Because I haven't been my best.

As if you'd heal my heart
And redeem the wrong I've done.
To forgive my foolish actions,
All for the fleeting fun.

I think I know it's you
And your presence calms me down.
Yes, I know I must come clean,
To live without this frown.

SALT & LIGHT

The Weight I Want

Thank you God for my precious cargo,
Whom I carry in my heart.
They are with me every step I walk,
No distance holds the power to ever do us part.

Both of my blood and my choosing,
These fragile items stored with me,
For whom I would take a bullet,
Chase danger, give my life up readily.

Oceans may, one day, fill the spaces
Where our bodies did coincide.
Still, as the salt will ever be in the sea,
So shall they, in my heart, reside.

Thank you Lord for my precious cargo,
The family and friends I've been blessed.
My own set of angels,
Who will haunt my heart until it rests.

Home

don't worry about me mama.
you've done the best, as you should.
I put my life in the hands of a Father,
whose will is always good.

don't worry about me mama.
I know, it's not all about me.
but, I'm trusting in a Father,
to put his trust in me.

don't worry about me mama.
I promise,
I will be alright.
and even when I'm gone,
thoughts of you
will drown my sight.

Mom & Pop

Strong are the wings of those
Who shelter others.

Brave are the hearts of those
Who care for others.

Blessed are the souls of those
Who know not

The great impact of their love
On this world.

Soul Sisters

I may not be able to teach you
To fully grasp your worth,
As a daughter of the King,
A princess since birth.

But I can give you reminders
And hope that you believe,
As I try to reiterate that,
You're more than what you see.

Your crown may slip
And tears will fall,
But be steadfast and mighty,
Stand firm and tall.

You're a woman of the world,
A sunflower in the field.
You're a diamond in the mine,
Such great power you wield.

Fix your gaze on your purpose,
You were sent here to soar.
Break your land locked chains,
Long for freedom no more!

I may not be able to teach you,
How to fully grasp your worth.
But, dear daughter of the Most High,
You are Heaven here on Earth.

Brothers & Sisters

We are petals & you grow next to me
A blossom doesn't blossom without the sun to set it free

We are fish & we swim in synchronicity
The water doesn't run without a little room to breathe

We are notes & we play in harmony
Without you, I sound as if something's off key

Comet Girl

Alana said she's out of style.
Been sitting plain for quite some while.
But her gears won't stop turning
    And midnight oil won't stop burning.

See, Alana may be out of fashion,
But she's searching for true compassion.
Haven't seen it in a minute,
    But sure is sweet when she's in it.

Her dress is plain and monochrome,
The voice of an angel is monotone.
Neurons firing out of sight,
    She's simple but out of this world, alright.

Roots

My roots,
Are fighting through the dirt.
My mother's roots,
Are fighting through the hurt.
My grandma's roots,
That hold us down
Are the deepest roots in our old ground.

In an ever changing world,
We're a mural of modernization.
How can we sit back and watch with elation?
As a treaty breeds tribulation
Between culture, tradition,
And this "great nation."
In development and housing,
We work to survive and still give praise
To the one who wakes us,
On these hard days.

My dear cousins, like raindrops,
With pure hearts of gold.
Rich in melanin,
Clothed in bold.
Shameless and proud,
Misunderstood.
Hawai'i sure is paradise
But search the shadows, if you would.
Take a second look on the streets
And at the children on the bus.

Sifting Through The Sand

Can we find peace?
Can they become us?
Take care of each other and end this friction.
A fire slowly smoking,
In the mix plate pot we're fixed in.

My roots,
They're tearing out of the dark.
My mother's roots,
Hear them singing in the park.
My grandma's roots,
Chuukese grace,
Waiting for balance in a blessed place.

Ai Tong Ngonuk

Don't call me a Micronesian princess,
Because she lives in a tent.
Her mother and father can't afford rent.
She's 9 years old,
And I don't understand thirst.
Most Micronesian kids, at lunch,
Always finish lunch first.
She taught me how to say
"I love you" in Chuukese.
When I found out she was homeless,
I felt my heart bleed.
When I found out she was blood,
I nearly fell to my knees.
It shook me for good,
I know I'll never be the same.
We don't deserve not to feel her pain.
I've been so lifted,
But was brought back down.
See, where I grew up,
We're the only ones in town.
Because they take up space in Kaka'ako
And you watch them fill our streets.
Still, I hear the most hurtful things,
So be weary who you meet.
Because this Micronesian is listening
And I forgive you, I do.
But there's a Micronesian princess,
Hungry and alone,
Who's listening too.

Be Blameless

Walk blamelessly in the world
& you'll walk with a world of companions.

Gifts

You're either granted a gift,
Or in the process of opening one.

The kind that may take years to find,
Strength to build,
And courage to express.

Be Water

Be Wind

Become From Within

The Savior Sail

Steered by the celestial sphere,
By help of Hōkūle'a and Hōkū Pa'a,
A cluster of eyes sailed to Tāhiti
On the ever graceful wa'a.
Navigating through the eternity of blue,
The crew held steady
Upon a voyage raw and true.

Now, around the globe they glide,
With a dream in their hearts,
Of reviving cultures and restoring
Long, lost survival arts.
Traveling across open waters,
Like the dove who flew out too far,
Blessed and faithful.
Trust, as bright as a star.

Little islands on a big planet.
Warrior hearts with no resistance.
Saving supernatural secrets,
While their light shines a great distance.

The more we advance,
As an evolving human race,
The more we come to realize
We're far past the need to slow down our pace.
Our choices have led us astray, far off the trail.
Only by ancient ways of nature,
To the future, we will sail.

Sifting Through The Sand

The children of Oceania
Now carry a destined calling,
To bring us back to our true selves
Before our impending falling…
Thus, these wayfinders, they inspire.
They instill hope with humility and love.
Hōkūle'a, her purpose,
Is sent from above.

His Land

Maybe Hawai'i was blessed with natural beauty
Because they overthrew the Queen.
Now of it's people are
Creators, change makers,
And all artists in between.

As the clouds glide by,
Watching over these people of the sea,
I'm reminded of His power
And never ending activity.

The mastermind of all creation.
The great, the only one.
Who penned
The galaxies,
The planets,

Hawai'i,

The moon,
And sun.

Promise

The world is my canvas,
My words are my paint,
My pen is the brush that colors my brain.
You may see me struggle
But you'll watch me try.
Then you'll read my lips,
While I touch the sky.

Innocence Is

When you think like a child,
You don't think about whether you can or can not.
You stand on the ledge with faith,
You jump, believing you'll be caught.

When you think like an adult,
You overthink the what ifs and what nots.
You stand on the ledge with your worry,
You somehow never jump,
Standing in the same spot.

Every Second You Are Born

Sometimes it isn't until the miraculous occurs that we
Tear down our walls of judgment
And allow ourselves to see the world
With an open mind,
With all of its beauty.

However, we must try to remember,
Miracles happen in every single moment.

It's Simple Pt. 2

He understands that the actions of one,
Has repercussions felt by many.
Eyes light with passion,
When he speaks of something he loves.

He notices the discrepancies in human nature
And tries to outweigh them with his love.
And every single being has beauty,
Some just need nurturing to let it show.

He takes injustice against himself lightly,
For he knows it's a weak moment of another.
Forgives, because he knows,
Life is much too short to hold grudges.

He is someone that I can look at and say
"If I ever have a son, I want him to be like you."
A man who does all this
And doesn't put it into words,
Giving me the greatest muse.

Garden Of Love

Don't pick flowers for me,
Tend to my garden.
Hydrate my roots,
Be the beg to my pardon.

The sun to my petals,
Energy to help me grow.
Give tender, patient care
So you may reap what you sow.

Don't pick flowers for me,
But work on them night and day.
In what you give your time,
My love will repay.

Can't Spell Shame Without Me

I don't know why I was made me this way
Or why my surroundings affected my persona so wide.
I don't know why I feel so hard.
These feelings, it feels, never subside.

I don't know why I was blessed with anxiety
Or caring about how I look.
I should love to love me,
Like I love a good book.

The reasons, I know, He must have His
But sometimes I fall back
And wonder, why all this?
And why me?
Dare I question the King.
In my heart, I know,
He has promise to bring.

I am sorry,
Don't blame me.
I don't fear the judgment of others,
Only I can shame me.

To Love

I am not my body,
This flesh I tend to see.
I am not my blemishes
And the shame I once believed.

Allow me to disrupt your world,
To remind you of what God can do.
He made man walk on water,
Float on treacherous banks of blue.

I am not my trembling voice,
Or my repeated sins.
I am not my fingernails tracing back to chaos,
That used to make my mind spin.

Allow me to shock your contentment,
To remind you of what God can do.
He made me love myself again,
So that I may love you.

Sky Bird

In tragedy,
There comes a moment when the tears stop
And the commotion ceases.
What happens next, though we cannot fathom,
Is ordered by God.

You see, getting burnt to ash and laying still,
With no pulse,
Has it's beauty.

A new being begins to emerge from the ashes,
And power sent down from the Heavens,
Brings dead bones to life.

Little by little, a bird evolves and matures,
Getting stronger each day.
She watches.
Observes the world with a silent mind.
She, perched in peace,
Let's the world do it's thing around her.
In a sudden revelation, she decides to

Jump.
        She soars.

She breathes in the air of the new world placed
Before her and flies through it's white clouds.
The bird knows not yet why she can,
But believes she was meant to do so.

Age

I asked God,
I thought my tough times were over?
And I think He said unto me…

"You're only 23.

This is an invitation.

You wouldn't be having
This opportunity for growth,
If you didn't have much more life to live."

Closing Poem

For too long, you've invaded my brain.
Thinking of you occurred like the water in rain.
Clouds in my head, you were all I could see,
I had to remind myself to look out for me.
In my faults and mistakes,
I ask for forgiveness, in time.
My past will always be a mess
And often out of line.

But once again, God wins.
With his blessing in disguise,
Through the anger, the fear, tears and the lies.
He's been knocking on my door
And it's time I let him in.
I'm no longer attracted to the confusion in sin.

Your love and your company,
I'll always adore.
If we can, one day, be friends,
There's nothing I'd love more.
I only want to encourage you
To make your future worthwhile.
And as I pray for you from a distance,
I'll be remembering your smile.
The one, I hope, never ceases to exist.
Here's to your health, peace, safety,
& a bond that will be missed.

Be Tideful

Your thoughts are like the tides,
So be mindful of what you make your moon.

Zoetic

We're looking at the same night sky,
You and I.
Searching for the stars
And the messages they may send.
Looking up,
Sorting out the means to our end.

Don't think, though, that this is small.
Because, here, right now,

It is all.

Relationship,
With the One
And all the others,
Is why we're called to be
Sisters and brothers.

When you seek,
You always find.
When you search,
You always see.
Shooting stars are everywhere,
If you want them to be.

Close to nothing can calm an angry man
Like God in the sunset can.

Universal Greeter

Harden not your heart.
Soften your brow.
Pause and let me wrap you in the now.

Harden not your heart.
Wrinkle because you grin.
Pause and let me take you in.

Harden not your heart.
Let down your hair.
Let me show you how the world looks,
When you become aware.

Tune In

You know that feeling when you find good music,
That speaks to your spirit?

It's like *daaaaamn*!
When you first hear it.

'Cuz I smile so big and nod my head,
The lyrics feed me like water and bread.

Thankful for the beat that set me free,
Like *damn*,

Did I find this music
Or did it find me?

God Loves These Songs

Here I fly, elevated.
Sitting with my mouth closed,
Concentrated.

As I sit here on this five hour flight,
Shuffling and saving,
I start to decipher,
A rapper's delight.

Buckled down with nothing more to hear,
Than the words they rhyme
Of love,
Of fear,

And of family,
Of life.
I smile to thank the man above,
For granting me this right.

Here I fly, on this plane,
In a romance with ART.
This catalyst of love,
Keeps humanity from falling apart.

Magic Made

From the weeds to the tallest branch,
Magic greens the land
In your fingertips and hands.

The currents and channels follow,
As magic steers the sea
From your toes up to your knees.

The sound in wind howls by
While magic holds those who fly.

It courses through your veins
And exists before your very eyes.

Relentless Resilience

Live relentless.
Failure isn't a word.
It's but an utterance of falsification,
Wrongful dictation,
It's not a word I think I've heard…

To me - To succeed
Is more than a win,
It's lessons, blessings, even
Forgiving oneself for one's sin.

It's not making a mill,
Or even a thou,
Shit if I needed to make a few grand right now,
I wouldn't know how.
But I don't feel like I'm poor,
I'm living lavishly at the bottom,
Anticipating the soar.

Failure isn't a word,
I won't let it exist in my vocabulary.
It's a misleading mistake of a word,
Therefore it is not scary.

Live relentless.
And don't forget to bounce back.
You might be swerving and curving,
But whose to say you're not on track?

Passion

Nothing you love will ever be a chore.
If you love it for real,
You'll always want more.

Senses

Who you are, you may not have meant to be,
Tread lightly, for the former is hard to see.

Those who find themselves when they choose,
Are the ones who seek to learn to use,
The connection between purpose and mission.
Find that His voice
Is the only thing you will hear,
If you listen.

Sifting Through The Sand

Think
Thought
As
Prayer

What He Likes About Us

He walked back inside from his mystic backyard that was only illuminated by the stars and that moon, his happy place if he ever were to choose one, I bet. I can only tell you so much as my words are pure speculation. I can tell you, though, that it was beautiful watching his journey play out. All humans have their quirks, their heartaches and their secrets.

This is what I really love about them.

The beginning of a story is the hardest part. This is what generates the angst and anxiety that every human knows all too well. Every action for every one is the start of a new page in their story, so they hesitate and ask "What if it turns out wrong?" Many of them don't realize it can never go wrong, but it will continue to be written.

This is what I really love about them.

Sifting Through The Sand

A dream without motion,
A candle without fire.

Wide-Eyed Wonder

Disregard whether or not it was written in the stars.
Your dreams limits are drawn like you are:

Full of possibilities that may seem out of reach.
Endless hope is something He's willing to teach.

Meet Me

Notice the patterns in art
And how we're but an art installation,
Put on display by our Creator,
To reveal His vibration.

Hear the waves as they crash,
Greeting shores with every stride,
Giving and taking,
Smoothing sands with their tides.

Feel the rhythm in the air,
Wings flying on invisible notes.
Art in everyday quiet,
Exposing blueprints that He wrote.

Inhale.

Exhale.

Sit with nothing of a plan.
And dare to comprehend the goodness
God has granted man.

Found

In admitting we are lost,
We are found.
And the joy of meeting placement
Is the most beautiful sound.

Frequencies of unseen magic,
A spirit of guidance in the night,
Provokes tormenting images
To flee our once tarnished sight.

Unknown oddities,
Throughout this world I was thrown in,
For me to uncover,
Reveal,
Drop to my knees
And declare, *You win*.

Prescription

May your health be determined by your will
 & your heart led by your faith.

Few and Far Apart

Dear God,
Save me from myself.
I'm falling into a strange depression,
Because even though I know you,
Something escapes me.

It is my ego
It is my *i*
It is my selfishness
It is a lie

You are the truth.
To you, I cling.
Hanging on for dear life,
My heart,
I now bring.

Wild Flowers

Some wildflowers live in the city,
Paying their debts,
While their souls do the bidding.

I'm told, wildflowers can't grow in the city,
And one wrong step
Can birth a world of pity.

So, if you see a wildflower,
Tell her kindly to go home.

>Your heart belongs to the Heavens,
>Not the streets you roam.

Reminders

God exists in growth when it rains,
And the light after a storm.

In peace after death
And broken hearts reborn.

In green mountains after a drought,
He succeeds through all your doubt.

In the color of shells to the tiniest fish,
He gives you shade with clouds
And stars on which you wish.

In your passion for that one thing,
And the worship that you sing.

You don't need to understand the world,
To understand who's King.

Here, On Earth, We Marvel

When you marvel at a piece of art,
Do you praise *it* or the creator?

For without he who made it so,
Surely, it would not exist.
And without the work of his hands,
All that beauty would go missed.

Still, surfers cherish the wave,
As the farmer with his land,
The wealthy with his money
And the famous with her fans.

But these blessings set before you
Are reminders of His grace.
His art here on Earth,
Of Heaven, a little taste.

Anela Lani

Why Artists Cry

Their songs are written in the depths of heartbreak
& poems are reflections of love long gone.
They put their every inch of harmony,
Into a simple song.

Their paintings are tattooed memories,
& the wildest of their dreams.
Their movies tell life,
Through eyes of supernatural beings.

Their books are childhood's past relived,
& stories never once told.
Artists cry to capture moments,
Both new and old.

They cry for injustice, poverty and the meek.
They cry because when beauty speaks
Rain falls from mountain peaks.

When I asked for strength to move rocks,
I began to move mountains.

7 Angels In Blue

This angel confused me but listened so well.
She did not judge and promised she'd never tell.
She told me I was insightful for so young,
On her promises, secrets and love,
She hung.

This angel gave me a warning to last.
She gave me an image I'll never get past.
She was so sure that she was okay,
But her demons resurfaced,
At the end of the day.

This angel belongs to someone I used to know,
She cared for everyone and watched us grow.
She had her trouble and a surviving spirit,
She was the laugh when you did not hear it.

This angel's young death shook the streets.
She had a twinkle in her eye,
A rascal smile when we'd meet.
She watches her friends in our home town,
Although she's gone, she still makes a sound.

This angel could not see with his eyes,
Yet he felt, he sang, and lived with surprise.
I was a child, so it's hard to understand
Why he meant so much,
But I love that he can.

Sifting Through The Sand

This angel is strong willed and brave,
She showed me that only God can save.
A spiritual connection is what we were deemed
And still, she visits me in my dreams.
She gave me a sister whom I'll watch after,
Whose humorous love brings us so much laughter.

This angel I love, could not walk,
But you could see her smile
And joy in her talk.
Chain smoked cigarettes,
Guess it runs in the fam.
Her son, my Pops,
One hell of a man.

Wind

There are these little things
That seem to speak to me.
You are the Universe,
I feel you in the breeze.

Now, I know
I'm not in control.
You've got a hold of me,
Now just mold me.

My Flightless Bird

We will not give up.
Flashes of moments when you aren't here.
Prophetic dreams.
Spirit sight seeings.
You might be well on your way,
But our mighty God is freeing.
We will not give up,
He is stronger than you.
With our heads bowed,
Unified as family, we might pull through.

I told you before,
I need you to see my first child.
I won't give up, it's not my style.
I might share this evil with you,
But I am no longer afraid,
I'm here to break the cycle,
Generation of newness, life remade.

Kindness in broken, tired eyes,
While your body lays in place.
A smile that makes me cry,
Soft but struggling face.

The most important part of our lives,
The giver with little words,
The reason we are who we are,
Thank you,
My flightless bird.

Imperfectionist

Throwing up my sins,
Thinking, *when will I learn?*
There's mold growing in me,
An unhealthy fern.

Trouble seems to be,
Spreading through my bones.
I'm surrounded by people,
So why do I feel alone?

A question marks,
The dying of my spirit.
A voice of uncertainty.
How can I trust my mind
And at the same time, fear it?

Shower baptize me,
Untangle my hair.
Bruised and abused,
I play stupid,
While fully aware
That

Depression is subtle.

Moment of Lament

Holy spirit, be my second skin,
Teach me to be tough.
Cover me in your security
Because this flesh has had enough.

Holy spirit, stand by me,
For my humanity bereaves.
These scars keep peeling open,
Bleeding, unforgiving maroon seas.

Would you just take over?
And may I give you all control?
Because this body's not doing so great
At housing it's very soul.

Grace

Grace saved me when I asked,
How did I get here Lord?
I put my body in situations
My soul couldn't afford.
And the price of my saving,
Was never too much,
For a Holy Spirit
Who heals with one touch.

Saved me when I thought,
There's no turning back.
There's no way in hell
I can escape this cold, dark, black.

Then I was snatched from evil,
Fought for my whole being.
I closed my eyes to the world and realized
Who I was really seeing.
The Spirit held me and my face got warm
I felt comfort, joy, forgiveness
And my tears brewed a storm.
I surrendered,
And I said, for the first time, out loud
I see you in every move I make and
In the world all around.
This is all yours
And I'm finally wising up.
You are the bread I will eat,
The water in my cup.

Sifting Through The Sand

Lead me, O Lord, for I will stumble and fail.
But your Grace, I now know,
Will always prevail.

The sun trusts the rain
Like His process trusts your pain.

The Harmony Concept

Observe it in the curiosities that make you wonder why.
The instances that bring you awe
And coincidences aside.

Watch it bring your day to end
And make muddy waters clear.
Experience deja-vu again,
Listen to what you hear.

Remember when it happens
And when you dream it in your sleep.
Recall life in moments of harmony,
The timeline of God's keep.

Genesis

I'm no painter
And cannot draw,
But this vision bestowed,
Leaves me in awe.
Of islands isolated,
From the rest of the land,
In the middle of nowhere,
Held in God's hands.

The ocean surrounds us,
Deep as the sky,
In His comfort and grace,
We solely rely.
Whether we're in four walls
Or on the streets,
Hear our cries,
For we're strong
When we're weak.

Then, ladders descend,
From East to West.
We call out His name,
In His house, we rest.
Across the isles
And through these aisles,
United, His love,
Echoes for miles.

Somebody

Wandering between two voices,
My thoughts and yours.
Confusion and questions,
Left me looking for more.

Then somebody told me,
That I'd be okay here.
Somebody told me,
I have nothing to fear.

But I didn't believe,
Until the day that you came.
And I didn't know you,
Until I met you by name.

See, I didn't believe,
I had my doubt.
What was this grace you were talking about?
I didn't see,
Holding onto old me.

Then somebody told me,
That I'd be okay here.

We, The Song

The composer,
With his right hand held high,
Lifts his staff slowly,
And lets out a gentle sigh.

He strikes!
Thunder roars.
The skies begin to shake.
He begins to dance.
The Earth begins to quake.

He teaches the choir,
"You can't misplace sand.
Wherever it falls,
I composed it to land."

The orchestrator,
Watches his musicians sway in song.
He feels their gratitude and passion
As he hums along.

Each of them, a grain of sand,
That can do no wrong.
Expressing themselves,
Exactly where they belong.

Victory

You are more than enough for me.
Give me Jesus,
And take everything.
Because all that I need is your love,
It's your love that sets me free.

When I'm drowning in my fears and doubts,
You come to me with your hand stretched out.
And when I feel that I've done all that I could,
You orchestrate and make things work for my good.

I have no need to fear,
Perfect love draws me near,
And by your grace you have made me complete.

When my rivers run dry,
And this world can't sustain me,
You are all that I need to get by.

Hope Army

Lord, undo the conditioning set upon me,
By the things all around me.
How could I have not seen
That my heart was betraying me?
Searching for tides of passion in all the wrong lakes.
Swimming in whirlpools of repeated mistakes.

In silence, I find your heart,
And you are much wiser than I…
Everyday, as I wake,
In your presence, I will try.

While the angels walk beside me,
With our shining shields on our chests.
The enemy loves to watch us question.
The enemy steals our rest.
He waits for his opening
In every moment that we breathe.
At our praise and renewal,
His evil stalks and seethes.

Battles in the spiritual realm,
Creeping into the physical.
We're no longer satisfied with the lie,
That this war is not mystical.
So angels, please walk with me.
We'll hold our swords out right and left,
Of your Word, in your glory,
For the Kingdom you have kept.

Sifting Through The Sand

Hope is the name of your army.

And we shall not be shaken.
The blows that come with battle,
Will, by God, not be forsaken.
Your blood's a saving sea,
That promised us life.

Hope, in you, Lord
Is why we fight.

Prayer In No Time

Give me strength.
Give me grace.
I trust in You
& live at Your pace.

Like A Flood

I prayed to be led by faith,
No longer by sight.
Nor emotion,
Nor fear of man, fight or flight.

Then, my cup runneth over.
It caused flooding through my streets.
It extended and invaded,
Carried debris far from me.
Wreaking havoc on my old ways,
A beautiful destruction occurred.
The answer to my prayers,
Were found in His Word.

Inviting a renewal,
He used His plans drawn out of dust.
And for this renovation of my soul,
He simply asked me for my trust.

Poetry & Saving

To salt and light,
I turn my head.
Committing to life
As I bury the dead.

Surrendering,
Your ocean welcomed me.
And I heard Heaven roar,
When we rose from the sea.

Sifting Through The Sand

ABOUT THE AUTHOR

Anela-Lani Elsie Alumbaugh is a Micronesian American poet from Honolulu, Hawai'i. Her mother is from the island of Chuuk and her father is an American, retired, U.S. Coast Guard lieutenant. She was born in Guam and has lived in several states but grew up mostly in Hawaii Kai on the island of O'ahu. She is a Henry J. Kaiser High School alumni and graduated with a Bachelors degree in Psychology and a Minor in Philosophy from the University of Hawaii at Manoa. She currently lives in Hawaii Kai. The next project she is working on is collaborative book and she hopes to continue to create in order to inspire individuals of all beliefs.

PHILIPPIANS 3: 13-14

PSALM 139

www.ingramcontent.com/pod-product-compliance
Lightning Source LLC
Chambersburg PA
CBHW071224090426
42736CB00014B/2965